Feelings

Proud

Sarah Medina

Illustrated by Jo Brooker

www.raintreepublishers.co.uk
Visit our website to find out more information about **Raintree** books.

To order:
 Phone 44 (0) 1865 888112
Send a fax to 44 (0) 1865 314091
Visit the Raintree Bookshop at **www.raintreepublishers.co.uk** to browse our catalogue and order online.

First published in Great Britain by Raintree,
Halley Court, Jordan Hill, Oxford OX2 8EJ,
part of Harcourt Education.
Raintree is a registered trademark of
Harcourt Education Ltd.

Editorial: Dan Nunn, Cassie Mayer and
  Diyan Leake
Design: Joanna Hinton-Malivoire and
  Ron Kamen
Picture research: Erica Newbery
Illustration: Jo Brooker
Production: Duncan Gilbert

Originated by Modern Age
Printed and bound in China by
  South China Printing Company

ISBN 978 1 4062 0639 5
11 10 09 08 07
10 9 8 7 6 5 4 3 2 1

British Library Cataloguing in Publication Data
Medina, Sarah
Feelings: Proud
179.8

A full catalogue record for this book is available
from the British Library.

Acknowledgements
The publishers would like to thank the following
for permission to reproduce photographs:
Bananastock p. **22A**, **C**; Getty Images/Asia Images
p. **22B**; Getty Images/Taxi p. **22D**.

Every effort has been made to contact copyright
holders of any material reproduced in this book.
Any omissions will be rectified in subsequent
printings if notice is given to the publishers.

Contents

What is pride? 4

What happens when I feel proud? 6

Why do I feel proud? 8

Is it OK to feel proud? 10

What can I do when I feel proud? 12

Will I always feel proud? 14

How can I tell if someone feels proud? 16

Can I join in when someone feels proud? 18

Proud to be proud! 20

What are these feelings? 22

Picture glossary 23

Index 24

Some words are shown in bold, **like this**. They are explained in the glossary on page 23.

What is pride?

Pride is a **feeling**. Feelings are something you feel inside. Everyone has different feelings all the time.

happy

sad

angry

When you are proud, you feel really good about something you have said or done.

5

What happens when I feel proud?

Pride can make you feel as if your heart is bursting! You may have a warm glow inside.

6

You may feel like smiling or laughing.
You may feel like hugging someone.

Why do I feel proud?

You might feel proud of something you have **achieved**. Doing something that you find hard always feels good.

You might feel proud of things you say or do, like being kind or helping someone.

Is it OK to feel proud?

Pride is a nice **feeling**. It is important to feel proud of the good things you do.

Don't be too proud, though! If you talk too much about what you have done, it might make others feel bad.

What can I do when I feel proud?

When you feel proud, tell your family. Put your work or prize somewhere you can see and enjoy it.

12

Remember, you do not need a prize to feel proud. Sometimes you can just enjoy being proud inside.

13

Will I always feel proud?

All **feelings** change over time. You might feel proud at first, and then forget all about it later.

Sometimes you will do something well, and sometimes you won't. But always feel proud of who you are.

How can I tell if someone feels proud?

When someone feels proud, they may look happy. Perhaps they have just finished doing something.

They may tell you why they are proud.
They might want to show you what
they have done.

Can I join in when someone feels proud?

When someone has done something to be proud of, tell them that you are proud of them as well.

When someone feels proud, they might just want to enjoy it quietly, by themselves. That's OK, too!

Proud to be proud!

We all have different **feelings** at different times. Feeling proud is wonderful. Enjoy it while it lasts!

If you ever feel sad, remember the times you felt proud. You will probably soon **cheer up!**

What are these feelings?

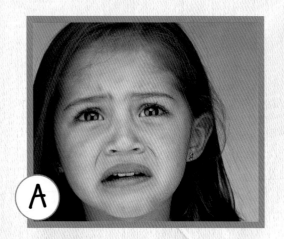

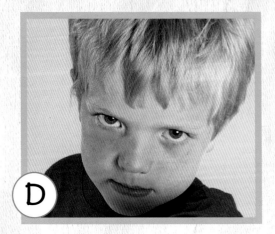

Which of these people look happy?
What are the other people feeling?
Look at page 24 to see the answer.

22

Picture glossary

achieve
when you finish something

cheer up
feel happier

feeling
something that you feel
inside. Pride is a feeling.

Index

feelings 4, 10, 14, 20

glow 6

heart 6

pride 4, 10

prize 12, 13

work 12

Answers to the questions on page 22

The person in picture B looks happy. The other people could be sad, angry, or lonely.

Note to Parents and Teachers

Reading for information is an important part of a child's literacy development. Learning begins with a question about something. Help children think of themselves as investigators and researchers by encouraging their questions about the world around them. Most chapters in this book begin with a question. Read the question together. Look at the pictures. Talk about what you think the answer might be. Then read the text to find out if your predictions were correct. Think of other questions you could ask about the topic, and discuss where you might find the answers. Assist children in using the picture glossary and the index to practice new vocabulary and research skills.

Titles in the *Feelings* series include:

Hardback 978 1 4062 0634 0

Hardback 978 1 4062 0638 8

Hardback 978 1 4062 0635 7

Hardback 978 1 4062 0637 1

Hardback 978 1 4062 0639 5

Hardback 978 1 4062 0636 4

Find out about the other titles from Raintree on our website www.raintreepublishers.co.uk